DON'T TELL
YOUR GRANDMA

DON'T TELL YOUR GRANDMA
YOUR GRANDMA
STORIES AND POEMS

Samantha Rae Lazar

ReadersMagnet, LLC

TABLE OF CONTENTS

ACKNOWLEDGMENTS

Thank you to the editors on Medium who
published versions of some of these stories and poems.

"All the Lies I Told Myself"- *Scribe*, May 18, 2021
"Unearthed"-*Blue Insights*, Dec. 20, 2019
"Regret Came to Meet Him"- *Parlor Tricks*, May 13, 2022
"This Involuntary Pirouette"- *Scuzzbucket*, July 4, 2021
"The In-Between"- *Scribe*, Dec. 27, 2019
"Just to Remember this Delicious Life"- *Scuzzbucket*, May 18, 2021
"When the Chimes Did Not Ring"- *Fictions*, Aug. 14, 2021
"Soon We're All Gone to Seed"- *Scrittura*, May 5, 2021
"Perception of Herself"- *Scrittura*, Nov. 29, 2020
"Antithesis"- *Scrittura*, April 24, 2021
"Reverse My Father's Ashes" – *Scrittura*, June 20, 2021
"A Lazy Witch Under an Aries Moon" – *Scrittura*, Oct. 22, 2021
"Inverse the Devil"- *Scrittura*, Sep. 20, 2021
"Find Release in the Thicket" – *Scuzzbucket*, Apr. 18, 2022
"Between Three Seasons" – *Scrittura*, Sep. 5, 2021
"The Risks of Playing in Nature" – *Scuzzbucket*, May 21, 2023
"My Body, Your Body" -- *Scrittura*, July 7, 2021

For Jason, who loves the dark with me but reminds me of my light

*"…And how Death is that remedy all singers dream of,
sing, remember, prophesy as in the Hebrew Anthem,
or the Buddhist Book of Answers—and my own
imagination of a withered leaf—at dawn—…a flash
away, and the great dream of Me or China, or you
and a phantom Russia, or a crumpled bed that never
existed—like a poem in the dark—escaped back to
Oblivion—…"*

— Allen Ginsberg, from "Kaddish"

THE BONES OF THIS HOME

what can be said that's never been told—a rock shattered glass and stayed—we played ancient backyards until you wondered about other things—we're a reality show documentary film crew and someone once buried a broken car under the invasive ivy—and I'm still pulling pieces out—rusted bolts and terracotta pipes—stashes of experimental moonshine —

the bones of this home were someone's post-war dream—landfills lived where someone slept—and the interstate was not cut yet—nor the smoke shop selling delta eight—nor the waffle house—nor picasso pawn—as if the surrealist would appreciate his namesake stamped on desperate sales, payday loans, or the bike I never recovered—all just stardust returned to stardust

the season changed when I was bargaining sleep for more time for me—the remnants of tulips now make way for early irises—I see the mess of winter—and I think maybe I could sweep it all into the backyard—bury it with the returning ivy I've removed barehanded—because I love the feel of dirt and work—vines as veins cycling through the days stubborn as blood

ANTITHESIS

this is not a poem, she wrote
pushed everything in, scraped buttons off the edge
sprayed the past year from her vacuum
took a short, soft look at it all
in the mirror with a mirror

this is not a song, she sung
the lowest notes made her high
that elephant vibration tried to send a message
it took a didgeridoo chirping savagely
on the back porch for her to misunderstand

I'm actually quite full, she shoveled
three more bites, a barista-cooked
lasagna over the fence
trying to attract the lost lovers
back, just to toss them aside

this is not a game, she won
the exact amount to pay all her debts
laughing out loud to earn the windfall
the world lined up to watch her
hula hoop, blow diamonds, and walk away

UNEARTHED

the dream again
variation on a theme
the backhoe comes out
to dig a grave for the pony

but it is not where I think
it should be

instead of at the homestead
it is next to my urban garden
remains of heirloom tomatoes
tangles of dried vines

I had planned to sow kale in autumn
a gardener's embarrassment

I didn't know we had people coming over
for my mother's pony's funeral

at first, I panic—confused about where the dirt
went from the digging
there was only a hole
with the cold body of the gentle animal

my son's first experience riding a horse
the patient eyes closed just gone
as is our ceremony

my shovel finds the pile and
I take my turn to help bury
and say goodbye

my eyes pan out
to the scene is a memory of another dream
real life or a dream or both
I awake with the fear of familiar

so close to where I hid something
too close to not have unearthed it

REGRET CAME TO MEET HIM

Regret came to meet him that Saturday afternoon, as he left the dry cleaners.

Will wasn't stupid enough to pretend he didn't know what he had seen in Tricia. When he had met her seven months ago, her self-righteousness was a huge turn-on.

***

While his mother's sign was the simple slogan: Life begins at conception, Tricia's read MURDERER in huge red font. She was the real deal, standing a foot over the legal protest line, heckling women as they parked their cars and averted their eyes on the way into the clinic.

It became a weekly date after that- Saturday morning protest, Sunday morning Church. Will felt powerful around Tricia. Their ideas caught on. Soon more people showed up for their meetings. Tricia wrote petitions, Will had them signed. It was finally happening. This case became the top priority at the highest levels.

Then one Saturday morning, Tricia asked Will to come over to her house after Protest. He knew she was particularly giddy because she had talked not one, but two girls into leaving the clinic. Her laugh made her beautiful, and Will felt an intense longing to kiss her.

She wanted much more than that.

"But we aren't married," Will insisted, ignoring the impulses of his groin.

"I'm on the pill. Don't worry," Tricia said, "but don't tell anyone." She pulled her dress over her head and tugged at his jeans.

Afterward, Will knew he would need to propose. He was flooded with thoughts of love and lust. He had never felt anything so good in his whole life. Guilt washed over him the next morning at church. He was positive the whole congregation could tell.

A week later, Tricia didn't show up at Protest. He didn't see her in her usual pew the next day. Three weeks went by, and Will could think of nothing else.

When he asked his mother if she had heard from Tricia's family, she said, "Oh Honey, they moved. Didn't she say goodbye?"

This realization hit Will in the stomach. He immediately went to the bathroom and threw up his Sunday supper. Heartache overtook him. The more he wondered about her, the more nauseated he became. His mother tried to comfort him, but he was lovesick. There was no cure if he could not see Tricia again.Every day he felt a little bit sicker, and he lost his appetite. Someone in his algebra class was wearing such strong cologne that he had to leave to throw up.

Then, the day they had been waiting for finally came. Roe vs. Wade had been overturned! All their hard work had paid off! Will just wished he could call Tricia and celebrate with her, but he didn't know where to find her.

He had started to get over his love for her, but his sickness continued. Everything seemed to get on his nerves. His mother especially. She insisted he go see a doctor. He waited another week and then made the appointment.

His doctor listened to his stomach, checked his blood, and examined him head to toe, but could not find anything wrong. Then he decided to do an ultrasound. He numbed Will so he would not feel the probe in his urethra.

"You're not going to believe this," his doctor said, "you're pregnant."

"I'm what?!"

"You have a fetus, look here." The doctor motioned for Will to look at the monitor, "and listen. Hear that?"

Will heard a rhythmic swishing sound. "Is that a…"

"A heartbeat, yes."

"But she said she was on the pill. She said it would be ok."

"No, Will. You are pregnant."

***

There were videos on how to perform the procedure. It seemed simple enough. Will drove himself far away from the city and to the meeting place. They had said to bring extra hangers and bottles of whiskey.

BASEMENT

After Ruth Porritt's "Read This Poem from the Bottom Up"
--This poem is to be read both ways.

Staring into the dark
You remember you're
Trying to feel the flick of fear
From the laundry chute of grandma's house
The bottom basket holds what's
Never thought to air before
To rinse the secret from the cloth
Three levels below folded dreams
Childhood ended through a creaking door
When looking up you saw
The light from where you came
Shining on what might follow you

THE HANGING CROW

there are many thoughts about the crow
they show up in my poems— thus, my dreams
patient on the gym roof spying
children leave behind everything

music still on my every breath
I follow the road to my family's place
a neighbor's rusted fences bark
still tout campaigns for trump & pence

watch on the right, my sister says
for there from a post, a crow is hung
and now its death won't leave my mind
and why the rope and why the gloat

some use the scarecrow arms out wide
the fields of precious lifeblood law
I expect an eye at the window/door
crosshairs for a trespasser

I'd like to make the heartless cry
but not to hurt or harm the man
more with a journalism bend
for when was last felt happiness

when was your soul last touched
from art, music, or poetry
when did your muse finally show up

and known, your tears, a chance to heal

did your mother kiss and sing to you
sweetly help you drift to dreams
if you can remember true connection
release the crow, the dove, the wren

MOLLY

Saturday: time for the Lake Swim—We would swim all the way to Bragoneer Dock- get Oreo cookies and swim back—one mile total. You had to be in Intermediates to do it, and Molly and I had a swim goal. Back in November we had emailed a pact: On the first day of camp, we would pass Advanced Beginners and go at once into Intermediates. That way, the Lake Swim was ours to be had, a rite of passage, a transition out of being baby campers. Those who had tasted the Lake Bragoneer Oreos were on a pedestal, and this year—this summer, we wanted a taste the first week.

We totally passed the swim test, and those kids who hadn't yet scowled at us. Maybe Lucy and Shannon would pass the next session. Molly and I high fived. We were in.

They made us wear orange, fluorescent swim caps for safety. And the row counselor would only use the motor in case of an emergency.

"I am not sure I want to go," Molly told me at breakfast. We had to come to the dining hall dressed in our swimsuits. She was wearing hers, but also one of those colorful sweaters from Guatemala. I wished I had one of those sweaters.

"It's really cold today," I said.

"It isn't that. I just don't feel good." Molly scratched her neck and pushed her cereal bowl away.

"Come on, Molly," I whined, "We have waited all year for today."

"I know, I don't know what is wrong."

My eyes widened and I looked directly at her, "Did you start?" We were ten, but Molly wasn't as flat as I still was.

"What? No!"

They always made a big deal over the "Guppies"—first time Lake Swimmers. Carlos was the row counselor, so he called each kid up one by one in front of everyone to honor them with their new swim cap, while the whole camp cheered, "Swim GUPPY, SWIM!"

Hearing Carlos call my name was an embarrassing and exhilarating initiation. I took my spot next to Molly and the other five new Guppies. I looked over at Molly- she was being so weird today. I knew she was nervous about the challenge, but she was opening her mouth and then closing it, over and over- sort of like she wanted to say something but decided not to.

The challenge of course, now that we were Lake Swimmers, was swimming the whole mile. Plenty of Guppies had opted into the rowboat. There was no shame in doing so. Swimming a mile was not easy. But our email pact had stated: NO ROW!

"OK," Molly ran to the swim docks, "Last one in has to kiss Carlos!" She giggled and held her hands on her neck. I chased after her.

The lake was freezing! I could not believe it. I was shivering and so were all the other kids. Molly shrugged and got her head wet right away. Carlos was in his boat ready with his megaphone. Tina, our fifth-grade girls' counselor was swimming in the front of the group, and Ben, the sixth-grade boy's counselor swam in the back. We found a place in the middle of about twenty campers, ready to go get those Oreos. One more chant of Swim Guppies! And we were off.

We doggie-paddled for a bit, so we could talk. "Isn't it weird how some parts of the water are suddenly warm and then you go into a cold spot?"

"I don't know. Not really," Molly said.

Were we just drifting apart? Why was she acting so strange today?

"When we get up past that sailing beach, see up ahead?" Molly pointed, dove under water, then came back up, "I am gonna take off my swim cap."

"Why? We aren't supposed to."

Molly dove under water again. I could tell she had practiced swimming at the YMCA this year, like she said she would. I couldn't get my mom to join and then well, time sort of went by. I was lucky I even passed the test.

Now she came back up, but she was at least 15 meters in front of me. "Molly!" I called out to her. I squinted my eyes and saw she was parallel with the sailing beach. I was probably going to have to get glasses when I got home. I couldn't really see her. She looked almost transparent- like the water was reflecting off her. I did see though, her bright orange swim cap, bobbing and drifting as I approached the place where I last had seen her.

I waved my hands. Carlos was rowing way up ahead with the fast swimmers. I could see that he was laughing- joking around with Tina and some older campers. Maybe Molly had passed them underwater. Maybe she wanted to eat the first Oreos.

Still, it was so strange. Molly was never a rule breaker. I grabbed onto her swim cap and swam with it. I was getting tired. NO ROW! I told myself. Not that Carlos was paying attention anyway. If that was what it would be like to be a teenager, then no thank you. This Lake Swim was not fun anymore. Where was Molly?

I began to swim towards the back of the group. Maybe she had fallen behind and was back with Ben and the other kids who were getting tired. Why in the world would I swim back the way I had come? I turned back and I was alone. I knew the water was way too deep to stand here. An oil slick from a speed boat passed me and at once I realized where Molly went.

I never ate Oreo cookies again.

A LAZY WITCH UNDER AN ARIES MOON

I've got a long way to go to catch up with you—perhaps the breeze behind is a little cooler/a little less restrictive (racing again?) broken-down arches, and an aging favorite tongue—I need nothing of your attention, but there you are

waving two-handed at the summit/I see you, Honey. Will you do nothing but keep me awake? Let me read and breathe.

The second summer beats down, always rots the pumpkin lot, oozing sticky—and still, I scrape—I curl the meat, consider saving the seeds to roast/I'm a lazy witch, lacking a cauldron and not caring enough. An Aries moon on fire this week, still trying to drag me up that hill.

I don't need anyone to see that I'm casting spells of my own down here. It's the magic hour—and I'm melting lady's mantle with gardenia oil while the autumn mushrooms remind me to call you prolific.

THIS INVOLUNTARY PIROUETTE

you awaken to a house
purpled by the twilight
and the ceiling clicks from
its silver latch
fleshy webs blur and block
a winding coil crunching
three times like boots on gravel
before your eyes
rounded jaws begin to spin
a water wheel of singular
top of the scale notes
slowly at first, a familiar
but unrecognizable melody
comes into focus and it sounds
like childhood ending
melancholy and expectant
as a swing returns to dangle
on a rusted chain
the notes, so high begin
to clink faster, and you
clench your teeth into
a frozen smile, a permanent
wince from the tone
so close, so on top of you
smothering you by sound
and you finally have enough

momentum to turn away
you try to lift your hands
to cover your ears, but
they are already high above
reaching for the slanted stars
your fingertips, posed in an O
feel strung together, woven
by fibers that are of you but
seem all wrong, and you pick up
speed and see your feet from
some peripheral vision
you are on point, on point
maddening cramps
from toe to arch to shin to thigh and
is that a ballet outfit, a tutu

the tulle and gauze, the exact
shade of lavender you'd wished
your heart out for so long ago
the metal jaws face you again
churning, chewing, and a twist
you turn away by luck or fate
dizzy from this involuntary pirouette
just when the agony of being glued
weighs your soul against the light
the music cuts, and by a hinge
you are folded into peace
to rest in the darkness
of your carved wooden box

SHANNON LEAVES HOME

The sign made Shannon gag. The fact that her dad was so proud of being able to erect the damn thing, with a party and everything. So gaudy. It loomed along the freeway in front of her, a nightmare. That roach slashed through the O in their last name. Gross.

The billboard read, *80 Years Dead: Cortney Family Exterminators*

Yet, she couldn't really complain, could she? She turned on the heated leather seats in her new birthday BMW SUV. Being finally 17, she could drive herself away from the house and go on past that stupid sign.

She knew she would be late now. She'd left the house already running behind, in a huff, slammed the front door, even. Ahead of her now, brake lights appeared in the morning rush. Great, she thought, some texter trying to merge, probably. Shannon came to a halt maybe six cars before she could pass the billboard. She scratched her forehead. *80 Years Dead.*

The cars did not move. She would be late for her lit class again. It wasn't as if she had finished her final paper anyway. Mr. Johnson had come to expect lateness from her, but she didn't want to disappoint him again. Maybe if she got there a few minutes late, she could creep in undetected. Or if he looked down at her, she would tell him she was in the restroom, say sorry, and take her seat.

But still, the cars were not moving, and that damn sign. It was so tacky. She told her dad she was embarrassed at the ribbon cutting. Tasteless. A ribbon cutting. She had finally gotten the nerve to bring her feelings to light.

"Not now, Shan!" her mother had hissed. She had grabbed, clawed to hold Shannon's hand. Told her to smile.

Now Shannon thought back to the sharpness in her mother's tone this morning. A screaming match, but an argument Shannon knew she could not win.

"Look at your legacy, Shannon, this is all yours!" Her mother practically spat the words at her.

"I don't want it!" Shannon screamed at her. She hated her family's business and what they did. And she had a secret. She didn't tell her mom she had seen the roach again in her bedroom.

Now Shannon rubbed her forehead and picked up her phone. "Fuck," she said out loud. She knew other kids would be late too. Surely, she wasn't the only one stuck on 347. Going this way was a mistake. She would get off at the next exit and make her way to school. She texted Nina: CALL ME.

Maybe Nina was late too or would step out of class to call her. It was now 8:15. She was officially late. But just five more months and then graduation. Hopefully.

Her guidance counselor had warned her last quarter. "You're too smart for this, Shannon," she'd said, "even if you plan a gap year, it will be harder for you to get into a good college. Your grades and recommendations matter. Your parents' influence can only go so far."

Shannon resented this, but she knew Ms. Collins was probably right. She could always just work for her dad, taking appointments, and doing filing and paperwork. She hated taking calls. People were frantic about bugs. They wanted advice, they wanted infestation to go away. They were always so grossed out when they called. It stressed her out. She knew she would have to work this summer anyway, when she wasn't retaking French 3 and Trig, the two classes she couldn't pass even if she begged. Would they even let her walk at graduation?

Her phone buzzed, and Nina's voice came over the speakers, "What's up, Heiress?"

"Shut up."

"Where are you?"

Nina had been at the ribbon-cutting, and she teased her now and then about Shannon's dad's speech. He had shown Shannon off, while her mother told her to smile. He called her the heiress. So humiliating. He always trapped her like this. Afterward, Shannon had cried about it to Nina, her longest friend.

"It's like you're in a Roach Motel," Nina said.

"You're not wrong."

Now she whined, "I'm stuck on 347! And oh my god, Nina, right under THE sign."

"OMG, that's perfect!" Nina laughed.

"Can you just tell Collins? Or tell Mr. Johnson, OK?"

"Just ditch," Nina said.

"I can't, Nina. I have this final paper. I'm kind of trapped."

"I'll tell him. Gotta go."

Shannon thought she should have just walked away when her mother guilted her, picked a fight with her. She turned the heat off and cracked the passenger side window. It was getting so stuffy in the car. Her forehead was breaking out, she could tell. Pulling down the mirror, there was a rash right above her eyebrows. Probably stress.

Someone behind her laid on their horn. What an ass, she thought, where can I go? She understood the sentiment though.

Her Waze app just noted the heavy traffic, but no updates, and no reason. *80 Years Dead*. Shannon felt a bit dizzy. She turned the radio on and could only hear static. She tried Spotify, same thing.

Maybe she would leave her SUV there on the freeway and just walk, but it was freezing out. She picked at her forehead and noticed two blackheads were blistering above each eyebrow.

She realized that in her hurry to get out of the house and away from her parents, she had forgotten to wash her face and take her medicine. This always made her sweat. Some sort of withdrawal side effects? She didn't know.

She opened the glove box. She had meant to stock her new SUV with extra Boron Wipes and a stash of pills in case this happened. She rummaged through her purse and backpack. Nothing.

"Stupid!" Shannon yelled at herself, and she pushed heavily on her own car horn, twice. Next to her, a kid in a white truck met her eyes, and he gave her the finger. As if she had cut him off, crashed, and caused this traffic jam.

She pulled her mirror down again. The blackheads started to erupt. It looked like two hairs sprouted out of them. She would pluck them out soon.

Shannon glanced over at the white truck again and accidentally caught the kid's attention again. This time he put his finger down his throat like he was trying to make himself vomit.

What the hell? she thought. She wouldn't be able to go to school today now. Even if the traffic cleared, she would have to turn around and go home to take her medicine.

She should have told her mother about the roach in her bedroom last night, but it was bad enough for her to fight this morning, she couldn't take anymore screaming.

The last time her mother had found a roach in the house, her scream could have woken the 80 Years Dead. She had woken in the night and gone downstairs. She saw one roach in the pantry and startled Shannon and Dale. They were caught. Dale, her parents' favorite employee, was trying to sneak out of the house. Shannon would never forget the look on her mother's face when she blamed her and Dale for the roach.

That was the end of the affair that should never have started. She had only been 15 then. "No bugs in my house!" her mother screamed at Dale. She had actually grabbed a butcher's knife and thrown it in his direction.

Shannon's mother had ignored her for two weeks until their next shipment of pills arrived. She knocked on her door, handed her the pills, and said, "Never speak of this." Then, to Shannon's horror, her mother tried to hug her, but they were too hardened against each other to ever have a hug feel normal.

Her father, however, just spoiled her rotten after that night. He gave her extra allowance, let her buy whatever she wanted. He seemed to forgive her for sleeping with Dale, and maybe he even took responsibility for it.

Now, she felt like she was being kicked out. She hadn't shown enough gratitude for the BMW. She hadn't been able to smile at the ribbon cutting. Well good, she thought, she wanted out of the family business. It could rot.

She wished she knew what happened to Dale after that night. She had really fallen for him. He had a protective shell that she loved. Sure, he was married already, and what they did was against the law. But why didn't her parents press charges?

What had she overheard the night after she and Dale had gotten caught? Her parents had fought.

"He knows!" her dad pleaded.

"What if she is pregnant? Then what?" her mother cried, "It's rape!"

"He knows, Morgan, he knows." Shannon's father seemed to have begged her mother into silence.

She hadn't gotten pregnant. They had been careful.

She wished she had gotten pregnant, run off with Dale who would have protected her. It would have been hard, but she knew she would never run that business.

If this traffic moved, Shannon decided she would go look for him. She would drive and drive and drive. Suddenly Shannon felt starving.

She saw a few fries on the floor, probably a spill from her McDonald's run with Nina last week. She snatched them quickly and gobbled them down. She needed more food.

She unlatched her seatbelt and crawled to the backseat. There was the pizza box she had tossed in the back. She was planning on throwing it away, wasn't she? Jackpot! Frozen lumps of cheese and cardboard. And a whole piece of crust!

This would satisfy her until she could get home. Then a wave of shame rushed over her. She glanced out the back window. The boy in the white truck gaped at her. He was pointing at her. His mouth was wide. She could see his tongue.

Shannon ducked back down beneath the window and searched the floor for more crumbs. I could get used to this, she thought, searching for crumbs will be the mission of my gap year! She felt the rumblings of the SUV's running motor on her belly. So what if he was pointing, she thought, hardening her feelings.

Then the guy behind her honked again. There was suddenly a chorus of honking. It startled her, this sudden noise. The honking screamed in her ears. She peeked her head over the edge of the window again. The white truck was gone. The traffic was moving!

She crawled awkwardly to the front seat of her SUV. Again, the guy behind her laid on his horn, and would not let up until he found an opening to pass her. She needed to get going. She needed to get out! But she couldn't get her hand to put the lever back in drive.

In fact, she couldn't find her hands. Spindly dark legs flailed in front of her. Two more legs poked through her coat, right at her rib cage. It felt almost relieving. The tension was leaving her body. She didn't really care about any of it, but she couldn't stay in this position. Her legs involuntarily scrambled, trying to turn her over to her belly. She did it. She turned correctly onto her six feet, belly down. Safe. She could do anything now.

Shannon felt herself crawl. Her feet gripped the cold glass of the window. She was up to the crack and felt the winter air on her face. Cars honked at the running SUV below her. She took one last look at the billboard, then raced for the sewers underneath it.

ONE INCH FROM BEING A CASUALTY

it was a back seat kind of impulse
the kind that inhibition mocks—
rolls its eyes and walks out on you
good luck with that, it says

fingers jammed,
not actually trying to make you feel good
just poking
and you don't know you are being molested,
but you do

it's over before it feels familiar,
like the memory of how a hangover tastes
it's a raw, real, fall-down laughing kind of sickness
telling someone to pull over now
and let you out

you couldn't handle that kind of party
it wasn't a fun pull to the lungs
and the mixture
didn't find you pretty

squatting shamelessly on the lawn
or off the roof of the house
one inch from being a casualty

immortality was a melting steering wheel

driving towards headlights on a one-way road
a gasping for help, for change, for luck, for another chance

it was knowing someone in school
who hanged himself
the curiosity of the trauma
could that have been you finding him dangling
could that have been you screaming for help before vomiting

then looking up and seeing his Converse high tops
a foot off the ground like a hovering hummingbird with
shoes
still but furiously moving at the same time

drained, gone, someone's baby,
someone's boyfriend, your lab partner
an empty seat in chemistry class
this time not skipping school
not offering you a taste-test of his latest dose

you do the work for both of you
measure, observe, collect data
excel, because you will—
get the hell out of this town

BLOOD LINES

This time when she runs away, she's passed by an open bed wagon with a red, white, and blue bumper sticker- "tired of the wreaked havoc yet? If not, you're not paying attention." She walks down Cross Plains Old Hwy 7; she has not seen her ride yet, so she keeps walking.

At first two Belgian draft horses are pulling the wagon but there is no driver. Swords are plunged into a few of the hay bales. She counts three ornate handles.

"The czar's soldiers," she whispers to herself.

The open wagon spits hay off the top pile, Alex blinks, shielding her eyes from the impending allergy attack. She sees blue eyes staring at her under a bale of hay. One horse snorts and slows long enough to pull its twin to a walk. She tries to get on- to get quicker passage to find her real ride- she is not sure which one this time, but a hand comes out from the bottom of the haystack. Not a gesture of wanting help. It's a warning.

A larger hand pulls him back into hiding, but a folded piece of paper floats from the wagon and lands at her feet. Alex takes it and reads the note: **I'm your great uncle.**

Another person to save, she thinks and begins to chase the vehicle which she realizes now is a truck speeding up. Diesel coughs in her face, her backpack bangs against the small of her back, and she leans over to catch her breath. The truck moves on and disappears over the next hill.

THE RISKS OF PLAYING IN NATURE

Do you think he will recognize my head?
The one which (if plans work)
will hit the floor right before set break.

Bets are:
It will bounce fiercely like the ball which
shattered my grandma's garage window

Others wager, likening it to bowling–
the clapping of pin against pin
the collapsing of towers
making league champions
out of my volatile parents
while I sat transfixed in the playroom
listening to the caregiver introduce Shel Silverstein
My sister thinks the POP will be necessary to vocalize
as dandelion blooms don't give like a cork
but more like a paper tear–
bitter and potentially poisonous
the risks of playing in nature

But removing my head will do nothing of those proven traits
of separation, release, and collision
It will operate out of its own set of elements
and other-worldly laws of physics

If I have it my way, the timing will be perfect.
One twin will watch his brother push for the bar
during second-set tuning–
a trick taught by their father,
other than the one where you just hand the hostess a hundred
in order to skip the line–
entitlement has yet to meet an uncrossable boundary

He'll trip over my head, while distracted by the lights of
the soundboard
nosing too close so people will think he's with the band

And my eyes will open, glowing blue from the floor
like icy vapor
my hair still wet from last week's rain
my lips still raw from his stubble

And he'll cry out in recognition
and maybe that will teach him
the meaning of consent.

MY BODY, YOUR BODY
OR HYPER-EMPATH'S REVENGE

After Octavia Butler

my body is your body now—no, you don't own me—it's not like that.

quite the upside-down concept, my secret—perhaps you've been burned

scars to the heart harden, not heal. wounds to the flesh aflame

fresh pain with each barometer change. or is it age? unrequited everything.

bones, organs, joints even react to the decision to wake up.

my body, your body—each place that took the brunt of your weapons—

your harsh tongue, your abandonment, your bruising hand, your indecency

caused a new kind of scar, a powerful scar—with mechanics

I myself can't understand—built from some ancient dark magic, metallic glittery and beautiful bead-like buttons emerge from the places of hurt

I've become quite shimmery, freckled with power, and I will let you

press my buttons, play me like a wicked melodica, and see what I can do.

I hope you have a high tolerance for pain.

CAPE SOUNION DREAM

Blue. She's a mermaid on stage, silhouettes of scenery, a shadow dropping sorcery into the impossible blue. She's prescribed travel notes and a searcher's companion—cliffside on Cape Sounion, she subscribes to the cult of Poseidon, imagines the drift of a parasail, and if she just goes Doric, everything will click into place.

It's here she's haunted—an Aegean wind whirls Attican sands from the rubble, compresses centuries of limestone passed hands—ships prepare for shore, whip up news of Pericles. She can hardly bear the beauty, swiftly sees tragedies—prickling imagery of souls diving toward the endless blue.

She's forgotten her devotion, gulls screech—seems a scolding, but she's entranced by the blue and the awe of the walls reshaping, reversing the ghosts of ruin. She feels it flutter—solar plexus—she realizes to pay close attention. It rises as one chakra and replays the history of lost control. Blue.

MEET ME AT THE INTERSECTION OF OPEN CARRY AND HEARTBEAT STREET

The victors (the vipers) wouldn't know Karma if they saw her in the mirror. Dystopian tunnel-visioned powers sling gold frisbees around an airy day.

At last, after a hard day's work, a holiday weekend to sit on their rotted laurels.

While they can holster their murder rods, I imagine myself a goddess mother of the pregnancy wand. I drive my all-wheel-drive solar, and wind harnessed energy bus (because who would trust that grid) and gift urine strips to all. Just meet me at the intersection of Open Carry and Heartbeat Street.

While this magic vehicle is almost invisible to the hypocritical eye, the inside is lush. Welcome to the safest of all liminal spaces. In here you heal. In here you decide. In here, you can get an out-of-state ride.

ONE PERCENT

"Everyone meets online these days," Melanie said.

"I know, but this seems way more complicated than using Match or OK Cupid." Lauren sipped her coffee and laughed at Melanie. She was always trying to set her up!

"Just try it- I know it seems a little scary, but it really isn't. Actually, I have found my real matches here. I mean, you don't want to meet up with just anyone, do you?"

Nodding, Lauren avoided eye contact with Melanie.

"Besides," Melanie said, "You can just delete it, if you don't pass the Portent. But I know you, and I know you will get in. You are one of us."

"What do you mean?"

"Just download it- Numinous- look me up on there- I'm Melonius17. Then let's talk about it next week."

"OK."

"I gotta go." Melanie poured the rest of her coffee into a travel mug. Lauren watched her friend disappear down the block, then down the steps to the subway.

A chilly spring breeze rattled the branches. The patio was filling up with students and friends meeting for breakfast, and Lauren felt pressured to give up her spot. Her waiter kept looking at her. Was she going to order anything else? Yes, she decided. She would order an omelet and toast and another coffee. The waiter glared at her but turned to bring the carafe and take her order.

Lauren typed in Numinous on the app store. The search circle spun for minutes before landing on an app. She had to use the fingerprint pad and Eye-scan to download it. Was this the Portent Melanie was talking about? Probably not. She had to use Eye-scan for banking, and a lot of apps used the fingerprint scanner.

"Welcome to Numinous," scrolled across the screen. Lauren read the instructions to allow the video to open and to use headphones.

Her omelet arrived, but she wasn't hungry anymore. The waiter sighed and brought her a takeaway container and her check. Lauren thought it might be better to do this at home anyway.

At home, she still was required to use headphones for the Portent. Lauren lived alone with her cat, Simone. The cat darted from the room the moment Lauren tapped on Numinous.

Settling into a turquoise velveteen chair, Lauren watched her screen come to life with voices and a swirl of faces on the screen. She felt dizzy until finally the face on the screen was her own, but it wasn't a mirror or the selfie mode on the camera. Her own voice spoke to her through her mouth on the screen, but she was not talking.

"Welcome to the Portent," Screen Lauren said, "the Portent analyzes your responses to some questions before connecting you through to Numinous. I will first begin to ask you to explain any supernatural or strange occurrences, mental powers, or attention to the occult at any point in your life. But first, do you have any questions?"

Lauren brought a hand up to her cheek and squished it gently to see if Screen Lauren would reflect back to her.

When Screen Lauren's face remained unchanged, she said, "It is normal to wonder why we use your own visage. This reflects your subconscious; however, you have complete control over how you respond. Think of it as your dream self."

How did Melanie? Lauren thought.

"You are allowed to invite people into Numinous if you are sure they will pass this Portent. Melanie was sure about you, even though you have not known each other that long. The more you connect on Numinous, the clearer it becomes who may enjoy our services."

"I noticed," Screen Lauren continued, "that you have the power to make people understand your needs without telling them. It's the opposite of mind-reading. You have a strong will, and other people respond to you."

"Telepathy," Lauren muttered. She thought of the times through childhood, how she had wished for gifts to be under her bed when she woke up. She felt if she bent her mind in a certain way, her mom would hear her. It worked once. One morning, there was a wrapped gift under her bed. It wasn't her birthday or any gift-giving holiday. Her mom had bought her the coveted Cabbage Patch doll, which was sold out at every store. She also remembered in high school, junior year, she could control how her teachers graded her work or left her alone when she was not in the mood for class.

"This is a powerful magic you have Lauren. You know this. You may encounter some problems meeting your matches on Numinous. Some people will be able to compete against your will with their own. Some will fear you. You may use this application, but training on mind control will be very important."

"OK," Lauren said.

"Unfortunately, the staff at Numinous has not completed the training modules for our consumers at this time. Hopefully you will find an apprenticeship with another member who can help you learn. I have clicked your first seeking preference for meeting others. As you begin to design your profile, other seeking preferences will come to you. Try not to go too fast."

Simone knocked a glass of water off the counter, startling Lauren. "Oh sorry, Kitty. I will feed you."

"Do you wish to continue?" Screen Lauren said.

This question repeated itself in Lauren's head. She dumped too much food in Simone's dish. She stared at her phone on the chair.

"Tap 'continue' on the screen to complete your enrollment."

Lauren paused.

"You may withdraw your enrollment at any time." Lauren's own voice no longer spoke to her. The voices began to mash together again, the faces swirled on her phone screen. It was someone else—something else.

Mark's text popped up on her screen.

I WILL BE OVER IN 20 MINUTES.

She couldn't get Mark to leave her alone. He just did not take a hint.

"The Portent will expire in 30 seconds."

Lauren took a deep breath and tapped 'Continue.'

SOOTHSAYING SILVERFISH

a glass noir—attempt to sleep and the same silverfish at
final rest at the base of peeling linoleum meets bath claw —
a reversed promise, as if this midnight post-coital toilet —
soothsays this—in a month a broom
will sweep away the lust
life will be lonely when he sets to clean the un-
mourned—will he notice what fragments of heart cover
the dust bin—will he finally see the silverfish?

driving out—superstitions, be trash— it's love's crushing
tides windshield wipers on high, week three—clean, clean,
clean and yet, the silverfish remains—a carcass, daring
depression to tear away my obsession with the bass of his
voice the arousal of his talents, the obsidian of his eyes

yet, the silverfish taunts and tempts past week four
settling in towards familiar—the waning crescent of our
honeymoon
and the floor seems set on the preservation of the dead,
and I see the bug has a new cocoon, bits of skin, and dust
and long-blonde hair—
decidedly not mine, nor his, nor ours

I tissue down around the dead, for the fish is mine to flush
his lack of housekeeping was almost forgiven
just as foretold, our month is up

PERCEPTION OF HERSELF

my grandmother was right
when you're dead, that's it
she was ahead of her time
that was the understood version
of who we knew her to be

but maybe she did not want
to be remembered
her own perception of herself
could have defied the conservation
of energy as memory

lifted away
thoughts like sheets flapping
on the line

just to remember her words
I locked them in with wax,
a transfer of heat
and determination

and I was dead-set
on knowing death
on knowing nothing
on feeling nothing
on feeling dead

I laid on the carpet
willing away the library ceiling
bright bulbs challenging my theory
I had the power to resist being created
at all

I had the power to flatten myself
against the earth
no teacher calling time
could destroy what
was never here
at all

even as weakened kinetic
energy, my father
squeezed my hand
transferring light to me
as he failed to breathe
my grandmother was wrong

CHORDS

how harmonious, we make blankets of each other, sneaking
off to higher mountains—windswept in the swoon—here
is the passion of earth—the wilderness of the never
summer—the stargaze of the Anasazi canyons—biking to
breakfast, he sings to me

he gifts me a new acoustic, pretends to burn his fingertips
on my shoelace
he says, sensuous. we read poetry and my life gets real
strumming elsewhere I lose my life before—here is a busking
companion, again—it's always the strings
we play soul mates for five days—romance the Bay of Biscay
strike the wrong chord, then separate ways

I'm tuning; he's listening to my aura
really I am running for the water
who can breathe in this heat

backpacker with a fitted guitar
he knows only now where we are
for romance is a train track and plucking a song I know by
heart

JUST TO REMEMBER THIS DELICIOUS LIFE

the eff. dee. ay. just approved
Rememeron™

a preventative and cure
for my age-old fears

perhaps it's in your family too
some tiny worm hungry for
short-term memory/long-term
recall/the hippocampus leaks

appointments first, then directions
home, then daily tasks
socks drop/a barefoot baby
faces are just faces who tell
stories of meals you made
and rollercoasters you rode
and shows you saw—front row
the love you gave
the cars you drove
and all the poetry—you wrote

to blank it all, life's cruel joke
and that is why I fear forgetting
and I downed this drug
twice a day, once for dreams
and once at dawn, but

read this carefully
I warn you memory is
only for those who can handle
the flashes of life not originally
built to last

the side effects of Rememeron™
are many, but may cause
a constant state of
Déjà Vu
flashbacks of the darkened nights
trauma memory (repressed)
trauma memory (treated)

memories of: being born, the time you peed your pants on the bus, shoved that guy (Chris?) at the bar, lies you told your mom, lies you told yourself (and the truths), the love you pushed away, the love that got away, the love that wouldn't leave you the hell alone, crashing the car, losing your tent, stealing some candy, ruining your dress, growing breasts, labor contractions, his first words and steps, dialogues as customer, the extra napkins you never brought to table 13, puppy kisses, virginity loss, rolling your first marijuana cigarette, drenching rain, saying 'I do,' campfire smell, getting lost in the great north woods, holding hands with the right person, to-do lists, pros and cons lists, playing mermaids, losing a love to the great Pacific, decisions that cannot be changed, going grey, losing friends, spinning dizzy, raspberry chocolate lava cake, people who don't recognize you or your name, heart-racing delirium at the top of a mountain, jokes and all the punchlines, recipes, throwing up, witnessing an act of love, thank you notes

you never wrote, splitting laughter and splitting pain, every
track of every train, and the sink, the sink forever full of
dishes, and one more thing: life. you will most certainly
remember life
the delicious, obnoxious,
heartbreaking, backbreaking,
precious memories
of life.

ALL THE LIES I TOLD MYSELF

My Dearest Miia,

To learn you are thriving and graduating from university makes me so grateful. I was fortunate to have been allowed to know about you and your life, if I so chose. However, I think it was probably ten years before I could accept the truth. By then, you were grown and living far from here.

I have waited years to find the courage enough to send a letter to you. In all honesty, I tried to forget you were mine. In the painful aftermath of our separation, I couldn't stand the thought of you having to see me caged, even more isolated than our cabin ever could be. And so, I told myself a story every day without you. In my story, it had been only your father and I in the woods. We were childless.

That was the easiest way to justify what happened to myself. At first, your father and I were deeply in love. We were so in love, we wanted to hide it away. We chose to isolate, and I did everything I could to make me love me, and you. There were signs, though. Days went by when I could not read him. He was unreachable. But he always returned to love me. I could not see his faults clearly, as if he was a sickness. He had a hold on me, and I was addicted to him. If there was a child, Miia, she was only in my dreams.

And my dreams were the truth. You carried that little bear everywhere with you. When we hiked, you taught it the names of all the trees and flowers you knew: rhododendron, poplar, sourwood, azalea, dogwood! You laughed at the "barking tree" joke and repeated it to your bear! I remember now, Miia. I remember.

As I tried to explain to the many doctors who tried to heal me, you never existed. They knew the truth, of course, but they played along with me after some time. They called me delusional and diagnosed me with some disassociation disorder. That was fine. My treatments and therapies and walks around the grounds helped me stop shaking after some months.

Yes, after you were taken from me, and I awoke from what I can only describe as a trance, I could not stop the tremors. It was if killing my husband and losing you caused some massive earthquake within me, and I was left with aftershock. I shook in every space inside me. My eyes tremored under their lids. My very scalp seemed to be shaking. Even after I was sedated, I shook and quaked in my bed.

I guess I was already well-practiced in my forgetting. I know you tried to tell me. Miia, I saw you whispering to your sweet teddy bear. I never listened when you told me what he did to you. I couldn't hear it. I was weak. I told you to go play, and I told you all the lies I told myself. Even the day we had to go to the hospital, your broken arm dangling like some marionette, I lied and told them you fell out of a tree. I should have protected you.

The trauma of the knife in my hand, your father's blood, your bruised face half-hidden in the doorway was too much for me to handle. I prayed that you could forget as well, even as you screamed for me, screamed for your teddy bear when they took you away.

I know now, after fifteen years, I could have healed faster. I could have allowed myself the truth. I might have been able to know you. But my love was so fierce, I knew I couldn't live if I allowed you to see me like this. I needed you to be free.

Now I have developed a cough that won't heal, and I have been given a grim prognosis. Please do not try to contact me. I have told my doctors; I will not see you. This letter serves as my goodbye to you. I wish it could be different, but I want nothing but peace for you in your life.

Please know that in the end, I was trying to protect you from your father. My own mistakes cost us our lives together, but I never wanted you to feel at fault. Please accept your teddy bear, enclosed with this letter. It is the only piece of you I kept. I wish you a beautiful, long life, that you so deserve.

Love forever,

Mother

YOUR ADDICTION WANTS
YOU DEAD AND OTHER WARNINGS

and why not watch it snow all night—the sound of static—the heat of reflection—harmonize with the old dial tone, hummmmmmmmmm —

and why not watch the next episode—the story carries you on the owl's wing—you've made it to western Utah on a bald tire before —

you've always quit before—the curl of smoke, the burn of it—eventually the ash of it—*your addiction wants you dead and other warnings*—a novel to break your wrist writing —

go ahead and call home—she said you always could—the phone, a wind-up toy—the cord is the right texture for chewing—and you have time to change your mind —

that tire's gonna blow and other warnings—a second edgy album to tear the drums pounding—you liked school too much to dare all the way—down the canyon where vitamins saved your soul —

FIND RELEASE IN THE THICKET

1.

we lunch with the devil's poetry lingering in the details
trying to find release in the thicket—a self-imposed cage
does pain make us insatiable or
is it the fear of feeling pain blocking the light of our own sun

everyone phases
and everyone stays in their decades-worn chair feeling the
pull
of forever—but I know we could never ride this transition
without holding hands

legs move, eyes lift, illusions of latches unlatch
we linger with the devil's poetry—moving is medicine
healing in the space of patience—muscle memory practice
until pain feels like something else altogether

2.

this plague is not over we spill wine drip
by drip
on the rims of our fillable plates
I drive around with a bag of food to donate
because her sign says, anything helps
honey, she says, I've got nowhere to cook

SAMANTHA RAE LAZAR

we're livin' in the woods behind Verizon and Play it Again
Sports

I could offer the eight-dollar-winning scratch lottery card
but that feels too much like second-place
and anyway, the light changes

REVERSE MY FATHER'S ASHES

this is fantasy, one that he would have liked, indeed—this
release we can't yet plan—and so a phoenix, caged he
remains —
in some twisted alchemy, I conjure us on the beach,
then the pier, then the rented boat that takes us at least
three miles offshore,
where legally you dump remains, deep Atlantic—

the ghosts of my grandpa and uncle, anglers in the
know—marlins, bluefins, seabass, grouper—they ride the
horizon, a Gulfstream duo.

we'd fly to Marrakesh, or row there, as would be his sense
of humor,
and the whole way:
Pete and Repeat went out in a boat. Pete fell in, who was
left?
trickster riddles charm their way.

it would be our family story, where we finally try to do
right by him, release the ashes to the sea, bye captain, but
the Wright Brothers' perfect winds still blow and shape
the dunes of the Outer Banks, and in a sadistic joke, a sea
breeze blows to reverse my father's ashes—

still shaking them out of the laundry, sticky and unwilling
to let go, ingested, a birthright tour.

or in another version, play the album backward
hear a devil's giggle in track one, the ashes swirl on the deck
rising to a flapping sail
cool almost to the temperature when he was coma-induced
ashes become genetic code, personality and memory,
and bone, sinew, muscle, organ, flesh, hair and clothes,
knowledge and humor and light, energy and relationship,
fatherhood and love.

a man on the deck becomes seasick, then finds his voice.

YOU PROPOSED ON OUR FIRST NIGHT

you proposed on our first night
figuring I would can our vegetables
and hold the fort
we'd set up shop in minion's field
spin medicines in homegrown
home-lathed mortars and pestles
you thought me, at once, the offal-type
pluck string and chord and envisioned me
with suede quiver over my shoulder
we'd homestead and traverse the earth
we'd watch each other growing older
you assumed me the goddess
of your manifest—
friends and family with the band

how fast you were to call us wed
as if I'd arrived dressed—gown and veil
when really, I had just escaped
set up my space, the sun had set
to the party late
barefoot, wiping back the tears
that drove me towards your proffered hand
that held the most majestic high
and sure, I'd be the queen that night
for us to dance and play enchant

the music carried forest blends
ravens, owls, and guinea hens
you invited me to meet your crew
around the brew, we struck the fire
your camper, though, I felt no
desire but to tent alone as I had planned
into my dawn without a man

you'd call me mornings after then
attached, you were so attached
and I knew I had for you no chance
you'd fallen to a bewitched state
to think I would be so fast to mate
so as your fate was broken-hearted—
for me, I told you, not to wait

WHEN WORDS ARE LOST

Calling you, change maker,
In your maker space
Come out, come out
Wherever you are,
And compose a breath
For all to take,

A dream for all
To finally awaken.
You can argue,
Not me, look away
And pretend this violence
Lives too far from home.

Compliance to the
Company that you keep,
Who pays someone else
To sweep your shame
Away, forgotten
Like the illusion of
Safety.

Again, wake up, you grieving child.
You were made to run.

It is, has been and will always be
Your discourse that we need.

Your voice for the future,
Stolen.

What word now, you speech weaver,
You diamond digger
You soul hider,

What happened after you promised
to lead?
And now to fight the bleed
The anger stuns,
And fear you eat
After which too full,
You drift back to sleep.

Calling you, the wisest one,
Removing your gag,
We're listening.
You were never supposed to
Silence your song.

Translate it quickly,
Melting weapons
Back to metals,
Where they belong.

THESE MYSTERIOUS MILES

Don't speed, my dad said—but I'm free—animated puppetry displays, ice cream spills on the parking lot—I'm the marionette in the glass case—I'm the rock holding a sleeping house—I'm the traveling raindrop, the round hallway holding many doors, the horizon of low clouds

I'm my sister's suitcase in the first row of feed corn—I'm also my mother's backpack, a puzzle box, a five-dollar bill on the motel's muddy ground—I'm the monster's heavy footfalls in my reoccurring dream

I'm the landing in the mansion of the cold ghost—a Poseidon cultist of the Aegean Sea—a cathedral's hollow space, the incense smoke of shared memory—I'm the risk taken for music over bald tires—I'm also the full moon pull and the double rainbow, the ditch catching a distracted driver

I'm the second-place medal—I'm the forgotten ticket, the turnaround, the love lost, the walk home, the broken pavement for sprained ankles, the broken glass in the back seat —

I'm the second decade, so far, of motherhood—I'm the rewind button of these mysterious miles—and I am the road.

WHEN THE CHIMES DID NOT RING

I waited, holding my breath at the mail slot. I thought I would hear the crunch of Stefan's gait up the gravel driveway, my cheek on the cold metal, a muddy finger or two pushing the rusty mail slot towards the room. He didn't come back then. He wouldn't come back then.

My sister, Lydia, called me yesterday. I told her that I really did not want to talk about it. No, not really. Not ever. I didn't want to tell her. But she acted like she already knew what happened.

I preferred my fantasy. You know, like when someone tells you to go out with this guy, and before you even know him, you imagine wine and farmer's market trips together, camping, and canning vegetables, laughter over the simple things. In reality, Stefan was a friend of my friend who warned me he had recently lost his wife to cancer.

I had been Stefan's first date since his wife died, and even though I knew he had something so heavy, I pretended not to know and hoped he wouldn't bring it up. I hadn't even gotten to the part in my meal where I could stop acting like a fourteen-year-old, when he told me about her and how nervous he was. But then I acted like I didn't know, or I tried to act like this news—this awful heart-wrenching news, was just news to me like I didn't know—which seemed so phony.

I am sure he could tell because he was wise. I was sure he was at least seven years older than me. Maybe he didn't notice. He seemed bored with me and my immature chatter. I drank that first glass of wine so quickly and ordered another. He kept looking at his watch.

That was the only time I went out with that man. I don't even remember his name. I couldn't fill the shoes of someone's loss. But then again, I tried.

This was a lie of course. This was the other story I told myself when I was out of love. When Stefan ignored me, or when he attacked me, or when he just couldn't leave me alone, I pretended he didn't exist.

Our marriage was, at first, exactly as I wanted it. I moved easily into Roberta's shoes. We wore the same size, and even though I sensed her watching me all the time, she could not actually wear the shoes any longer. She could haunt me though.

Every time Stefan came home, he sized me up. When we first got married, my hair was too short. He wouldn't touch me until it came down past my shoulders. I couldn't stand it. It was a stringy mess that I wore in a bun. He insisted I take it down, and he measured it. He used a tape measure. It took six months for my hair to be an appropriate length. Then we made love. He held my hand in public. Or rather he grabbed my hand tightly. He cuffed my head and sometimes put his hand on the back of my neck, pushing gently, but still pushing me along.

I saw Roberta in the reflection when I went to wind the grandfather clock. God, I hated those chimes, but he insisted on every 15 minutes. Every 15 minutes marked that many fewer minutes we had to be together. I had to make sure the chimes were accurate or else suffer. I saw Roberta twice there in the glass, long dark hair, deep-set eyes, pleading with me behind my watery reflection. If it wasn't enough that he made sure I was doing it right!

I told Lydia, "I don't want to tell you or talk about it ever!" Except she already knew. Did I tell her? What did I tell her? What did she say?

"It wasn't cancer," she had said once.

Another time, I called her, and my hair dripped slippery beads through the hallway. I knew she could hear my gasping, even though I said barely a word. That was after he tried to drown me. I knew he was in charge after that. I knew before the day at the pond. But that day it solidified.

Now I waited through the midnight chimes, and nothing came. Half-dreaming, I thought I heard the screen door being pulled and Stefan's hand through the mail slot. I slid to the cool tiles until I felt sleep overtake me and I woke to a slam on the back porch.

It must have been three or four—the time when the dew hadn't settled. I shined my flashlight into the mist off the back porch. The light reflected itself so I couldn't see where the sound came from.

Then, like oncoming traffic in the rain, I began to see a slow shimmer appear from the east field, walking towards me or rather gliding because I couldn't see any legs. I couldn't see, but I sensed it or felt it. Then I heard the slam again, against the back porch—it was off the side of the house now, on the wrap-around deck. I squinted back at the rolling mist, but I still couldn't make out a figure.

I turned off the flashlight, hoping to find relief in my pounding heart. A dog's barking from up the road bounced off the pond, and I felt sudden gratitude for the company, for the morning that would be here soon.

I turned back towards the house and realized I had left the sliding glass door open. I was also barefoot. I would have to refinish the deck. Splinters from dry wood poked at my toes, and I suddenly knew I had let it in. Or I felt completely awake to the fact that I wasn't alone. The dog barked again and then another one, the hound I recognized, Leonard from up the way. The dawn was approaching, but the sky was muddled and mostly gray.

I felt a chill from the damp air, and I decided not to go back into the house just yet. More silence. I realized then that the chimes did not ring. The clock needed winding again. I was so used to it, that I almost didn't notice. Maybe that was my mistake, but I decided that I was finished with that clock. I was going to live without that incessant noise. That incessant announcement. Time would go by either way.

I closed the door and pulled on my barn boots and set out to check for eggs. The graininess of the landscape was beginning to settle and soon I would see my chickens. I felt along the deck railing for my egg basket. It had fallen off the hook and lay soggy in the grass. The day felt off, and I tried my regular routine which would calm my nerves. Usually, my cat would come to greet me this time in the morning, but he was off somewhere. I would have to shoo him away anyway to feed the chickens.

I would have to tell Lydia eventually. Even if she already knew, she did not know the whole story, and I knew that no one, not one person, knew the whole story. I am not sure I even understood it all, but I surely knew more than anyone else. If I didn't call her back soon, well, I knew where that would lead. People didn't let questions stay unanswered, so they would begin to fill in the blanks. They would fill in the blanks with the worst kind of details—the worst sort of imagination that other people would agree to. I would have to call her back.

My sister did not understand my choice of life. She lived in a downtown loft and ate dinner out every night. I am not even sure she had ever invited me there. But halfway across the country—it didn't matter. What happened out here tended to stay out here. Except it didn't. I must have let it slip at some point. People can sense misery even if they don't know the details. Lydia never even saw my broken tooth. She didn't know my ripped clothing still lay in a heap in the laundry room.

The chickens were still nesting, and I could tell it was a timeless night. Like sitting on a bench all night outside the train station that time the sun went down very late, and we missed the last train. And so, no hotels would take us and so there we sat, pocketknives in hand. I was ready, even then. On those sorts of nights, the sun never seemed to rise.

It was too quiet at the chicken coop. Too quiet. Even for sleeping birds. I unlatched their pen and cooed, "Hey Maple. Maple. Shiny?" I knew the birds were not there. There were no feathers or chicken blood—some dogs got loose out here a couple of years ago and made a mess of my chickens, so I had installed chicken wire fencing, with a roof and everything. Maple and Shiny were gone. I turned towards the house, looming darkness—why had I not brought the flashlight out here? Where was the cat?

Back on the porch, I began to sing, "Pumpkin, here kitty, kitty. Pumpkin?" No matter, that little tabby had run off, and come to think of it, he hadn't eaten his breakfast. I tapped the edge of his food dish with the toe of my boot, the slide of the ceramic on wood was too loud for the stillness of the night, and I looked behind me to see if any neighbors were around.

The slamming. It happened again. I couldn't bring myself to check that side of the deck. There was no way Stefan could have scratched his way out. I was alone.

My reflection in the sliding glass door reminded me that I was not eating either. Me and Pumpkin, too disinterested in food today or yesterday or tonight or whatever time.

I touched the scar on my neck, my pulse, thick with anxiety, making the thin purple line rise to its original scab. The wound reversed itself. A slow trickle dripped through my fingers onto the deck. That is when I saw it. I had let Stefan in, and his scolding eyes burned me through the sliding glass.

He checked his watch.

BREED

In 1980 a boy
I will never forget
with a sneer of copied hate-
passed down from

Them
The deceived and deprived
Depraved blamers
pointed his finger
at me

Did he have an audience?
A cheering section
scared to not agree, no doubt
I was told at recess

I would be shot
for my ancestry

That may be my only
Memory
So stark from that year

Yesterday, my son
Same sweet age
I was then
He is now

History repeats, they say

And through the woods
They made a game
Of their *escape*

Evacuate
For some
Poisoned voice
called to exercise his right
to hate

Was this a call from my generation?
What happened to my first-grade bully—
Did he graduate or pull the alarm
satisfied by the power?

He could create *panic*

To calm our youth with no answers
We learn the past to not forget
To teach forgiveness in the face
of lessons we thought
we already learned

May my child and all the children
Remember *no fear*
That the path they walked
down this year
was only guiding them
to **love.**

STAYING TOO LONG: A LOVE STORY

after yoga class
he asked for her phone number
but warned her he would be leaving
in a month to teach in Japan
and that would be that

she was brave
she could handle not falling in love
or she could try and make him stay
she had the done the whole try to change and trap thing
more than once before
this time she wouldn't even think
about their life together in the future
she did not even make room for him in her house
they would not paint the bathroom red together
there would be no grocery shopping or sharing secrets

how they would travel the world

he had just ended a relationship
so did she, sort of

she loved that he lived in a tiny apartment
in a refurbished historic hotel downtown
he traveled by bike everywhere he went
his bicycle shoes clacked up the stairs to her apartment
his intelligence matched hers

on their first date he took her out for sambuca and rum balls
they both enjoyed a delicious appetite for sex and hilarious banter
about being teachers

she had a month
that was all
a simple timer on this relationship
it wouldn't be difficult to say goodbye
there was an exact ending

he was so funny
their friendship was obvious

their second date was a snow day
roads were icy and school was closed
she trudged up the street to get some coffee
feeling the glow she had forgotten could happen
she wouldn't get attached
her boots crunched and she kept her head down
the snow came down heavy and beautiful
and in this moment
she was this free spirit unattached

looking up the sidewalk, there he was

a coincidence
it was not fate
they were not "supposed to be together"
it wasn't that strange
the coffee shop sat almost exactly halfway between their
homes

meeting eyes, they both laughed at the odds
this would be their new favorite morning place

a few weeks passed
together almost every day
cooking, riding bikes around town and on the trails
driving him to work in the morning
strapping his bike on her car—the roof racks weren't just there
to look cool
he tickled her and gave her pet names

she wouldn't love him

one week left
"I'm not going," he told her
she loved him

the pregnancy, then
which had to end
when summer came
he left.

THROUGH THE ACHE OF THE SOMEDAY RAIN

I've got a low boil, slow boil ache—
the kind that stays supple in the Tropicana days
the kind that left me winded on the sidewalk outside
Jade Garden at 87th and Metcalf Avenue
half a mind to walk home in the flash flood splash
with no forgiveness in my heart
for a man late to meet his dealer
while I dawdle with the after-dinner mints dish and I'm
seven again
reading all the posters of the thirty-one flavors
skinned shins and dirt-blood knees
yes, that too
but please
give me some Advil
for the bruised bone
door slamming
the vacuum of a relationship
formed only by basement
apartments, school-skipping
nitrous-sipping, ashtrays
and almosts
your trauma and my trauma
were hanging up clothes
it's a bulging scar on my writing arm—
if it could be a soothsayer, it would tell of strength
even through the ache of the someday rain

WHISPER TRUTHS TO THE WINDS

To the keepers of knowledge and those who try to destroy it—I envision Mount Rushmore-sized erasers—soiled and sweating humanity ordered by (old white men) to scrape off their own history (both histories by default of the deed) —

I have some questions:

Who is this grand scholar who reads and curates what children should or should not know? Who are your puppeteers? Did you forget your sense of wonder?

Do you ever look up and ask—what am I made of? How did my own sacrifice bring me here? Do you ever consider your mother's pain upon bringing you into this world? Her body- your dependence, her sustenance- your everything?

Do you remember learning to read—the joy of inspiration, creation, and epiphany? Did you test out thinking for yourself—challenging your teachers—asking why?

Did you ever live a study of opposites? Run into the storm just to feel wet? Change your mind, cancel plans, regret your choice, try out a new genre, learn a foreign language?

Do you ever look at your empty bank account and then give gifts to those in deeper despair on your way to the next hustle? Did you ever pour your blood on the page only to be rejected but then resolve to try again?

Did you ever look into your lover's eyes and thank them for being the one person around whom you can be the messy, aging, exhausted, hopeful, lost, evolving, forgiving human you are?

Did you ever stand to watch the sunrise at the ocean's edge—lulled by the power of froth and crest, sandpipers dancing along, the squeal of thieving seagulls, a retired couple bending to seek treasure in a tidepool—and think I could die here?

Did you ever stand breathless after the final climb, giggling with oxygen-depleted euphoria, switchbacks as the snakes who brought you here, towns as miniature dreams, the mountain over a challenge for next summer—and wish to be born with wings next time around?

Who was your model for the normalization of trauma? Who decided your passion wasn't worth the pursuit? Who brings you a pillow before you reflect and what haunts your sleep no matter which house you inhabit?

For the humanity erasers, I have news for you:

No matter how hard you scrub, no matter how hot your fire, no matter which century you cover with your thickest paint, no matter how deep you dig—pencil lines are traceable, veneer cracks, bone shards surface, and ashes whisper truths to the winds.

TURBULENT DISCOURSE

what is the agitation about—tone, tact, timing
a turbulent discourse, or a four-course meal, she likes to stir
the cauldron
no eyes, all eyes, either way
a language playful, like a scratch-off game
bets on misunderstanding or wanting to know more or
walking away
digging too deep—marrow, crust, center of the Tootsie Pop
there could be something for everyone, if only for impatience
sleuthing for the other side, hiding all weapons
she holds opinions as dandelion wisps—full of fiction,
character, history, a full backstory, and lets them go—plenty
of weeds in the front yard
she's here for the banter, the labyrinth, the sound of your
voice
she's grown out of absinthe, but her mind could change if
only the right prompt came along, and she can be face to
face with the sun

WHEN YOU SEE MY EYES

I saw you, as old father, in the supermarket last weekend—my
sister never sees you old, Dad, as an aside—
you, as other man, half bent leaning, a steady walker driving
the cart, hair wild with sleepless sleep—
I think that is about right, I remember when I last saw you
well(ish), not intubated, not four levels below the surface,
begging lungs and heart and kidneys to dance back to
sustainable rhythm, not swollen and sunken,
not grasping for recognition in my voice — singing
Woodstock—*we've got*
to get ourselves back to the garden—
not wanting me to stop when you see my eyes are your eyes
not lowered by regret, but raised by the man you might
have been

I saw you again, as young father, while I slept—you a demon
telling me to kill you, that it was okay to kill you, that I could
do it—and I could not get lucid
enough to find your eyes that are my eyes and tell you
no—and so in braids I skipped down the gravel driveway,
looking for a burial plot—past the alfalfa
field—where the dogs had to go, not surviving the angry
neighbor's last straw.

I awoke with no power, frightened of my forewarning, but I
missed you die as I tried to write sky high, willing the flight
to get south quicker to

be there with my sister—yes it has been a year and two months—and what a year you missed, how you would have shook your fists to the planets—these politics—these viruses—your parents would roll over in their Chicago plots to see you now—we promise to get to spreading your ashes.

of all the things your eyes, my eyes could have seen, the travel of the well,
your days of baseball and a burned down home—a few miles from Lake Michigan—your wit and slow decline—you had always been this way, separate, removed, wanting to be known but not understanding how to know someone

open a wallet and see what remained of your life—our last text exchange—
I can read on your cell phone—suffering voice still saved on mine—though I let go of the childhood and the absence of you—these last days of your life hang on, like you did for too long—because love is like that.

SIXTEEN

Play with fire and laugh, fall on the floor, close to the singed carpet. She bleeds there too in the same space. Maybe it was her period, rubbing the hot spots raw, like a dog in heat.

High school, laughter and the dose slips off her mouth onto the same spot. Bragging that she's going somewhere else, try to find her, give her pets, like the poodle she is. Pick it up in a five-second-rule game, place it back on her tongue. Sniff the ground for spills.

How deep will she go into the opiate cave before she knows/cares something's wrong. And it is jarring enough for the insistence of that Dinosaur Jr. same song same song he insists must be on for the sake of all things holy turn it down/off. A girl's got homework.

There they are ditch witches, looking for the seeds. Crunching boots so satisfied by dried irises and fake accents. Escape is an exaggerated plan, because nobody really knows the way out.

BETWEEN THREE SEASONS

(a poem in three acts)

Act I: Mabon

[lights up on woman digging in her garden at dawn: soliloquy]

such is life in the later harvest
it seems I am too late
too obscure
for these fruits
yet, I dig
for what I've buried
yet, I dig
to plan deceit
either way—nebulous
why must I then
cover my being
protection is the illusion

what is hidden?
what is worth hiding?

[rainbowed dance on a cliff]

she sees no need
for the search
every beginning

holds all the truth
of a falling leaf
of a receding horizon
everything is behind
and everything is ahead
there is now
without ego
without regret
without an audience
she halts
then leaps

[woman asleep in a nest: meditation in silhouette]

an act of rest is vulnerability
but surrender is protection
the bough may break
but after the grand adventure
and a short slumber
she finds her center
and disarms the confusion
by showing her heart

Act II: Yule

[luna moth emerges from chrysalis: soliloquy]

I am humbled before the divine
emerged as forgiveness with wings
to see me at all is an act of healing
for we are symmetry, you and I
with the balance and humility

of knowing one's calling

this is the time to say yes
to yourself

[luna moth flies off, stage right]

[luna moth arrives at party preparation meeting: family is
frozen/thick with tension]

eye to eye
a pre-dated play
of the long-lined heredity
of the same-old dynamic

and she too plays a role
as peacemaker, as disassociate
her watchful landing
turns her into victim
accused of her beauty
accused of thinking she is above it all

when really, she just wants to help
and have fun
who will be the one
to break the trance

even if she flies back

to the iced-over garden
to begin the dig again
she will still be dancing
the dance

[woman pushes open the door of the ski lodge, she seeks the fireplace, sits down in the warmest place next to a beautiful man. A mirror hangs above the mantle]

are you the shaman, she asks
if you want me to be, he says
he puffs a smoke-ring
she tries to catch it as if a solid
but she's been here before
his eyes are so familiar
so enchanting

rising to go home
he grabs her hand
wait, he says
she pulls away
and heads out into the snow

Act III: Ostara

[lights up on woman approaching a bonfire at dusk, strings of fairy lights hang from blossoming dogwood and cherry trees, sounds of acoustic guitar and a familiar voice]

return. celebrate. toast
known, the fire's high
play. pretend. Imagine
strum to the night sky
laugh. live. emerge.
friends understand you try
love. keep. deserve.
the family by your side

[lights up on a lot of broken cups, spills, and remains of
debauchery—hangover: a song and dance of crawling and
sleeping and cleaning up the mess]

shall we survive our choices
shall we remember what was done
can we stop the bleed now
that we have let them in

[Dénouement: woman sits in meditation; birds fly and chirp
at sunrise over a wooded mountain]

she returns to the garden
there was nothing to hide
she's home here again
to sow seeds
for her future
for the amazement of spring
she's a goddess of Beltane
earth mother indeed

[curtain]

SOON WE'RE ALL GONE TO SEED

The Pavlovian chime, it's the countdown when you're not listening, on the third strike, fading, fading, fading, gone. Your screen should be closed. Your neck aligned with spine. Your life alone. Silence. Come out of your drool stance. Come away from your fixed meditation, ignorance, group illiteracy.

Some dogs cannot be trained, cannot be willed away from their obsession. Some salivate for the squirrel on high, a broken nest, the ghost of yesterday's chase. Senses dulled, a sound means nothing, a singular scent, the only synapse.

Ignored and back to the garden. Dirt on concrete, a purchase of canned compost, a larvae-food wood barrier, stretched thin hours, licking drips of salt, and soon we're all gone to seed.

How will I be received at the closed door? I can knock and scratch at the shutout. A brick through the lens of the attic, treading lake water with it, ten pounds, sixty seconds, hold it higher overhead. I'm a lifeguard now. Whistle, check.

NARRATIVE OF NECESSITY

that silver briefcase/attaché
wants nothing from me
remains in the trunk of my car
the storage unit in the driveway
fragments of pass-codes
hard handwriting, its own
printing press by the force
of trying to stop a shaking hand
an old deed to a Chicago cemetery
the plots sold or not I won't know
he wasn't interested in that reality
and a collection of keys
none of which open the story
I want to stop telling, anyway.

A KING WHO POISONS THE WELL

don't fear the thing
that's killing us,
says the leader
it's not really that bad

optics show and tell
this is how to be remembered
bravado shaking the handrail
a zoomed in white-knuckled grip
on his own reality:

he's off to bed
a king who poisons the well
and drinks to prove a point
this isn't sustainable
breathing in chaos

trapping it in fabric
what's mine is mine
everyone can do
what he enables and get away
with it, especially those
at his false altitude

that is the way then
a quick grab through
a smashed window

and really was it worth
a felony charge

for cigarettes—menthols!
and a case of beer
probably now, yes
at least potentially
the crime is worth knowing
what the wait is for—
thickening the file
our files are all thick

will someday this poem
or your poem be the reason
we press charges
some digital footprints

are waiting a reckoning
the cyber space we share
a jail cell for the willing
is she smiling
I cannot tell

who is she really anymore
people change in isolation
people change
when days on days
we're holding our breath

trapped in our own game
meanwhile, eyes dart
from grief, to compassion,

to hate, to guilt, to fronting
like we were never taught to read

BY ANY MEANS

Awake- concrete. The chain allowed the bathroom; the explosion of pain fogged every sense.

By any means.

Crawling, she spit blood; avoided mirrors.

His mistake: a phone left charging in the living room, out of reach, as if to taunt her. He would be back for it. Her resolve returned, sharp as the hidden metal. Swallowing four pills, she packed bandages, antiseptic, and his sweater.

Her body quaked as she grasped the last thing on her list: torn aluminum. Her hand– the only thing that stood in the way of her escape.

The door.

"Hey, babe, forgot my phone!"

SEVENTEEN

Let me tell you: Don't drop acid and go to Orange Julius before prom. Don't sit in the car until a security guard makes you go in. He won't care if your face looks like melting crayons. You will have a choice, but the obvious one: don't let him drive, so go in and get a photo taken. Ignore the other girls in the mirror. They may not understand the lack of white in your eyes. Hope the camera is forgiving. Don't be a demon doll and get all snarky with the DJ for only playing country music. You did not come to this country club to dance. In an hour, you'll make the midnight showing of The Wall over at the dollar cinema. A good thing to do next would be to have forethoughts so you can change out of that black number your mom loved on you in the dressing room. Jeans and a T-shirt in a backpack and some sneakers will do. It will be a tangle with his tux and your pantyhose in his Triumph, TR4, you'll joke is a Matchbox car. But it will be too much effort to take the roof down. The Pink Floyd movie will depress the hell out of both of you, but coming down, you'll make a game out of not getting off, grinding teeth, sloshing waterbed, fevered, and desperate all night long.

DON'T TELL YOUR GRANDMA

*

You are beautiful, she said. You are beautiful, he said. You are just so pretty.
Where did you get those eyes?

You want to turn your whole body inside out
skin in, eyeballs in
vessels and sinew and organs out
synapses seen.
That will teach them how what they teach you causes neural pathways to become
permanent impulses: wretched, sticky,
weathered trenches.

*

You are five, almost six. You know of the unicorn that taps on your window in the mornings. It lights sunbeams, begging you to get up and see. You can't get out of bed in time to visit your pet, but she is waiting.

*

Your parents go to dinner with your grandparents. You stay in your mom's childhood bedroom– silhouette photography, a scratchy coverlet, a collection of miniature eggs, and a

pattern carved into the wood. You trace the lines, a labyrinth spiral on a twin bed.
You suck your thumb. It's hard to sleep.
A boy you saw at Passover dinner babysits. Some family friend's teenage son takes his time, and you learn right from wrong by what he says before leaving the room.
When he rubs your back, you are a kitten-- like the new ones your cat birthed over the summer, so many sweet kittens. You want to purr and rub your back against his hand, and he slides it down to your bottom, under your pajamas, where he rubs and rubs;

You can drift like this. So when he says, don't tell your grandma–
all at once, you are not a good girl.
You are pretty; you are at fault,
and you can't sleep;
you wait for him to return
so you can ask him what he meant.

*

You are in first grade. You took a particular test that let you start Kindergarten before you turned five. You don't feel different than other kids, except for the mean ones. You would never play catch and kiss with those kids at recess. They are not even kissable anyway. You wonder if their mommies kiss them and tell them to say the worst mean things to you.

In your special class, you learn about the stock market. You choose Pepsi to follow for a while, but you would rather learn to paint with oils. You have this idea for a giant painting. You will need a ladder. It is based on this book you fell in love with and will keep forever. You will paint a woman with blondish-brown hair and big blue eyes who is you when you are old or maybe your daughter when she grows up or maybe it is someone from your family long ago. She rides away on the unicorn in the photo, rags hanging on her from the basement days. She had been tied up for a few weeks, but she sort of liked the feeling. They were monsters, all of them. They loved her, and even though they had power over her and did bad things to her body, she actually had the power.

*

Who is this man sitting at the top of the sledding hill? He drinks from a glass bottle, and you think his green eyes are made of glass; is he your mom or dad's good friend? He wants you to sit next to him on the grass, and the sun is going down. His beard is thicker than your dad's. It is reddish, and even though you are nine, you wonder what it would feel like against your face. You flip your hair so more people may notice the pretend dangles. You will get them pierced soon. You're old enough. He doesn't have much to talk about– this man at your parent's party. You wonder if you will think about him when he gets up to see what all the hooting and hollering is about, and you wonder if he will think about you as he crunches the gravel toward the weeping willow.
Hide and seek.

*

He likes that you're smart; you make the first move.
You want him to roll you off to squeal on his motorcycle,
take you home, and teach you chess before your mom comes
to get you.
He likes that you'll dare you, but you will go first.

*

You have a pink leather jacket and a 10-speed Schwinn
that's red.
In your neighborhood, you meet up with this kid who lives
on the other side of the canal,
and you sneak into the houses under construction. They
remind you of treehouses.
You love a good fort.

*

Your grandmother says, "girls your age shouldn't have love
handles."
You say, "Pass the pasta."

*

You'll fly to his homecoming in a couple of months.
You and your friends will rent an RV, and you'll avoid school
after dinner.
Instead, you'll try to hear secret messages in "The Great
Gig in the Sky"
and pretend you're drunk.

He'll want a repeat, but you won't let him get past your clothes. You'll roll on the carpet in the upstairs office all night. He'll beg like you're an expert, and he'll pout. You'll fade apart.

He'll hear that you have another boyfriend already, he'll cry on the phone and never want to talk to you again.

He will later confess he accidentally left the shoebox saved filled with your hand-written, long-distance relationship on the Greyhound to Chicago.

Please leave your message after the beep:
"We know where you live. We're gonna rape you."
If you were your mother, you would cry deep-rooted tears. The same, the same. You would blame yourself. Yourself. Your fault.

You investigate nothing.

You're in high school. You're immortal.

*

You sneak onto the golf course at night. Both couples. She seems to be into it because they've been dating for a year. But you are not sure, and you think you'll get caught. He thinks he is Morrissey. He does look like him, you admit. You like him a lot and know better, but you can't seem to break away. He mashes his lips to yours and pushes you onto the manicured grass. His tongue is Camel Lights. He's pushing into you, pulling at your jeans. You tell him no, but he has you pinned, and you give in.

The sprinkler system cuts on, you are drenched, and you are safe. He laughs for way too long. You guess he's good at pretending. You'll adopt this persona for a while.

*

His apology is white noise. At this point, you've tuned him out. All you want is action. He has left you stranded for the last time.

Fucking 87th and Metcalf before his stoned ass realized you weren't in the back seat. You imagine the laugh those two had, pissing their pants and turning the jeep around. You were paying the bill for those broke shits. And they just leave? Does he know what you would do to him if there were no tomorrow?

*

You pass the packs into the canyon—hand over hand, this adventure. You are so deeply in love. You are 20, and yes, this one started as an affair, a lie you could not keep for long. This one was real. This one would stay. Backpacking seals the wax. Seeing the sweat roll off each other's brows. Kissing the earth off each other. He's yours. He'll care enough to ferry you to your next chapter.

*

He says, "I know where you live because I've been watching you. I've seen you around campus and walking home." This is the last time you give your number to a random man on a motorcycle.

*

Picking up your pills at the pharmacy, Dad tags along on this errand before you go out for dinner. He asks the pharmacist if she thinks you are on a date.

*

You are teaching high school English. These kids don't want to be here. You're a newbie, and you can't make it fun yet.
This boy won't take off his Tennessee ballcap;
"Go Vols," he says.
Whatever– he is 16.
He blows kisses at you from the back row and smacks his lips over braces.
Your adviser tells you to dress differently: wear old-lady clothes.
You're teaching *The Crucible*. He tells you he knows where you live.
You call him an asshole—the class claps.

*

In Venice, one time, this guy licks your neck. He asks you to stay in Italy forever and work in his restaurant, where you decide it's a good idea to sip wine until past closing time.
He licks you goodbye.
Next stop, Rialto!
On the boat, two other men lick their lips at you. You are not food.

*

You wanted both babies. You just didn't want him. Or him.

*

Being ghosted is the coldest of cold, even in the strange warmth of North Carolina during a hurricane. One moment, morning rising in a threatening whirl of humidity, you are standing on a picnic table hugging him. You are taller now, his head against your chest. You hop down, and he kisses your head, holds your hand and tells you he loves where your relationship is going. The weather is changing, and you part ways for now. You are aglow from your night together. The grilled salmon, his childhood home, his baby book he shares with his mother's ancient creativity, the love. And the hurricane comes, and the man you fall for never calls you again.

*

Every day is a chance to start again. Even when the light's all wrong inside the tent, and you know you said no, but were too drunk to stop it from happening (again). You want him to be worthy. You want to go out to breakfast, but first, he must stop by his friend's van parked in a way-out lot of the festival. Other people are there too. He sells a variety of drugs. Like the ice cream man, he's a fucking vendor, but with baggies in coolers. You curse your life choices but still are hungry, and the new guy in your life doesn't seem to buy anything- just says hi, so ok, you can handle the fact that they are friends, you tell yourself. So you go to eat breakfast with him in town. He doesn't have enough money. So you pay for the food. And still, a week later, you cling to the maybe. The wish for him to be something other than what he is sticking to you, like the stink of the sleeping bag the next day.

*

This guy changes depending on who is around him. He is into some tai chi, and you think he's really into you. He also has it in him to be your personal trainer. He wants to train you. Asks you if you want flat abs. Good luck, you think. Also, you should ask him if he wants you to have flat abs. Asking you if you want a six-pack is like a backward way of telling you that you're not exactly right. Anyway- you will try this costume for a bit. You think he is Zen. Your performance arts and yoga teacher friend introduced you, so yeah. He is the second guy you have dated to have a nature name.

He is into Tai Chi and some other martial arts where he is training himself to delay ejaculation to build his chi. You don't really get it, but you buy him a silk scarf that he will use to tie his testicles. He is methodical about many things, and you are not sure. He comes to your birthday party and gives you a buddha statue. You start to fall for him a little. You enjoy that he wants to pleasure you, but you don't understand why it can't be mutual. It is off-putting. He tries to control your breathing. Comments on the way you express pleasure. He is fascinating and terrifying. You find his weak spot a few weeks in: alcohol.

You go out one night after hanging out with some of his friends who own a skate shop. You are wearing one of your favorite dresses. It is black and swingy with tiny white polka dots. You basically adopted the dress out of your sister's closet. You wear it with your Frye boots and a sweater, and you love it. He tells you never to wear it again because it hurts his eyes.

He drinks a lot with these friends. Some band is playing, and you tell him you are going to the bathroom. It is one stall, and when you go in, he follows you. You laugh a little, but there is this look in his eye. You sit down on the toilet, and he's in front of you, unzipping and holding your head to him. Luckily, he's drunk enough to lose balance when you shove him away and leave him there in the stall.

*

Wrap up all these endings.
Send them afloat-
see if someone adopts the basket of goodies downriver.
Let them make something beautiful out of all this.
Decades remind you that you're always you,
but it's hard to believe the chapters written and still not written are also you—
your ten-year-old is asleep.
You roll over and tell your husband your lost babies would be 21 and 19 now, grateful he can follow
your midnight train of thought.
His arms fold around you– tuck you in, safe.

THE SUBTLETY OF SEPTEMBER

I walk about my life
on the 2nd of September
unburdened
because it's Dad's birthday
but it's his unbirthday
his old phone stays charged
in my desk drawer

September sneaks in
as August's softer sister
wise from the strain
of breathing
like a loblolly pine
choked by kudzu vine
suddenly cut free

as we pass through the
summer of the year
we hoped for normality
we can't change the equinox
but we can accept change
even if we don't notice
time slips, we slip
we arrive

within the subtlety of September
slanted sunlight

SAMANTHA RAE LAZAR

casts sparkle on a mourning dove
on the powerline
still my favorite birdsong
neeee woo woo woo.

LEAVE IT EMPTY

I.

For the one you cannot forget, until your life leaves you alone. For the bruised bone, they told you, takes longer to heal than the fractured bone. Feeling the rain coming over the mountains, cleansing the door frame, blowing steam on the windows of the basement apartment you barely escaped. But still the rain, a reminder you got away, drenching, beautiful, thunderous rain.

II.

For the survival of loss, crusted over, picked apart. For the canyon that blooms wildflowers in the unseen crevasse, it is best to leave it empty. For what fills it, unmonitored, is excessive longing for anything to fill an unfillable gap. Beauty is contained in the open box, in the box of boxes, in the nest you've built, in the sacred space.

III.

For the inside out and long way home, circles and cycles of people and dreams. Characters out of nowhere, your teachers arrive, and the decomposers clean, and blisters burst golden relief.

Printed in the USA
CPSIA information can be obtained
at www.ICGtesting.com
LVHW041326141023
760904LV00007B/779